D1121642

BUFFALO YOGA

BUFFALO YOGA

Charles Wright

Farrar, Straus and Giroux / New York

Farrar, Straus and Giroux
19 Union Square West, New York 10003

Grateful acknowledgment is made to the editors of the following magazines, in whose pages some of these poems originally appeared: *The American Poetry Review, Field, The Oxford American, The Yale Review, Poetry, Hotel Amerika, The New Yorker, The Roanoke Review, Hunger Mountain, The Yalobusha Review, Meridian, Ploughshares, Shenandoah, Appalachian Life, The Southeast Review, Pagine* (Italy), *Five Points, Oxford Poetry* (England), and *Bluesky.*

Library of Congress Cataloging-in-Publication Data
Wright, Charles, 1935–
    Buffalo yoga / Charles Wright.— 1st ed.
        p.   cm.
    ISBN 0-374-11728-4 (alk. paper)
    I. Title.

    PS3573.R52B84 2004
    811'.54—dc21

                            2003054702

Designed by Jonathan D. Lippincott

www.fsgbooks.com

10   9   8   7   6   5   4   3   2   1

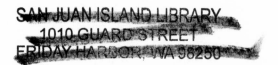

For Holly, heart-string and harp

Contents

PROEMS
Landscape with Missing Overtones   3
There Is a Balm in Gilead   4
Portrait of the Artist by Li Shang-Yin   6

BUFFALO YOGA
Buffalo Yoga   9

BUFFALO YOGA CODAS
Buffalo Yoga Coda I   25
Buffalo Yoga Coda II   28
Buffalo Yoga Coda III   31

SNAKE EYES
The Gospel According to St. Someone   37
Homage to Mark Rothko   38
Portrait of the Artist in a Prospect of Stone   40
Rosso Venexiano   43
Words Are the Diminution of All Things   45
Arrivederci Kingsport   46
January II   49
Dio Ed Io   50
Nostalgia III   52
In Praise of Thomas Chatterton   53
Charles Wright and the 940 Locust Avenue Heraclitean Rhythm
      Band   54

Saturday Afternoon   56
Wednesday Morning   58
Homage to Giorgio Morandi   60
Little Apocalypse   62
Snake Eyes   63
My Own Little Civil War   64
La Dolceamara Vita   67
Sun-Saddled, Coke-Copping, Bad-Boozing Blues   68
Sinology   70

POSTSCRIPTS
Little Apokatastasis   73
Star Turn III   74
In Praise of Han Shan   76

Notes   77

PROEMS

Landscape with Missing Overtones

The sun has set behind the Blue Ridge,
And evening with its blotting paper
                                    lifts off the light.
Shadowy yards.   Moon through the white pines.

There Is a Balm in Gilead

Crows in a caterwaul on the limb-laced edge of the afternoon,
Three scored like black notes in the bare oak across the street.
The past is a thousand-mile view I can't quite see the end of.
Heart-halved, I stare out the window to ease its medicine in.

———————

Landscape's a local affliction that has no beginning and no end,
Here when we come and here when we go.
Like white clouds, our poems drift over it,
                              looking for somewhere to lie low.
They neither hinder nor help.

———————

Night sky black water,
                    reservoir crow-black and sky-black,
Starless and Godless.
Cars trundle like glowworms across the bridge, angel-eyed,
Silver-grilled.
            The fish in the waters of heaven gleam like knives.

———————

I write, as I said before, to untie myself, to stand clear,
To extricate an absence,
The ultimate hush of language,
                        (fricative, verb, and phoneme),
The silence that turns the silence off.

———————

Butt-end of January, leaf-ash and unclaimed snow,
Cold blue of blue jay cutting down to the feeder box,
The morning lit with regret,
No trace of our coming, no trace of our going back.

Portrait of the Artist by Li Shang-Yin

My portrait is almost finished now

in the Book of White Hair.

Sunset over the Blue Ridge.

Puce floating cloud.

A minute of splendor is a minute of ash.

BUFFALO YOGA

Buffalo Yoga

Everything's more essential in northern light, horses
Lie down in the dry meadow,
Clouds trail, like prairie schooners,
                                        across the edge of the left horizon,
Swallows jackknife and swan dive,
Bees blip and flies croon, God with his good ear to the ground.

Everything's more severe, wind
At a standstill and almost visible in the tamaracks,
Golden sap on the lodgepole pine
                                        mosaicked and Byzantine
Inside the day's cupola,
Cuneiform characters shadowed across the forest floor.

Everything seems immediate,
                                        like splinters of the divine
Suddenly flecked in our fingertips,
Forbidden knowledge of what's beyond what we can just make out,
Saw grass blades in their willingness to dazzle and bend,
Mnemonic waters, jack snipe, nightjar.

———————

God's ghost taps once on the world's window,
                                        then taps again
And drags his chains through the evergreens.
Weather is where he came from, and to weather returns,
His backside black on the southern sky,
Mumbling and muttering, distance like doomsday loose in his
      hands.

———————

The soul, as Mallarmé says, is a rhythmical knot.
That form unties. Or reties.
                              Each is its own music,
The dark spider that chords and frets, unstringing and stringing,
Instrument, shadowy air-walker,
A long lamentation,
                    poem whose siren song we're rocked by.

———————

An article isn't the last word, although we'd like it so.
Always there will be others,
                            somewhere along the narrow road
That keeps on disappearing
                          just there, in the mountains.

———————

As soon as I sat down, I forgot what I wanted to say.
Outside, the wind tore through the stiff trees
Like rips through fabric.
                        The bored hum of a lawn mower
Ebbed and flowed, white horse standing still in the near meadow,
No word in my ear, no word on the tip of my tongue.
It's out there, I guess,
Among the flowers and wind-hung and hovering birds,
And I have forgotten it,
                        dry leaf on a dry creek.
Memory's nobody's fool, and keeps close to the ground.

———————

All my life I've listened for the dark speech of silence,
And now, every night,
I hear a slight murmur, a slow rush,
My blood setting out on its long journey beyond the skin.

Earlier lives are restlessly playing hide-and-seek
Among the bog lilies and slough grass.
In this late light, the deer seem a sort of Georg Trakl blue.
The pond dims, the lonely evening pond.
A dead face appears at the window, then disappears.
The sky returns to its room,
                              monk birds pull up their hoods.

This is how the evening begins,
                              arranging its black pieces
Across the landscape.
Enormous silence, like wind, blows south through the meadow
        grasses.
Everything else holds its breath.
Stars begin to appear as the night sky
                              sets out its own pieces, the white ones.
Its moves are not new, but they are inexorable, and cold.

———————

The sun, like a golden octopus
                              out from its reef
Of clouds, or the clouds themselves, so transubstantiationally strange
In summer weather,
Or what's left of the evergreens in their stern vestments,
It's never the same day twice.

A poem is read by the poet, who then becomes
That poem himself
For a little while,
                              caught in its glistening tentacles.
The waters of deep remembering
Wash over him, clouds build up,

As do the shadowy pools
                    under the evergreens.
Later, the winds of forgetfulness
Blow in from a thousand miles away
And the poet starts to write.
This is the way the day moves,
                    and the sparks from its wheels.

He didn't have much to say, he thought,
                    but knew at least how to say it.
Cold comfort. Sunday,
The clouds in their summer whites,
The meadow a Paris green,
                    black and tan of the trees.
Sundays are no good, he thought, Sundays are all used up.
Poor miter, poor chasuble.

Mondays are worse still. Tuesday's the one,
                    inanimate Tuesday,
So gentle, so pacified.
They flutter like flames, like feathers, from the brown calendars of
    the past.
Each of us has his day when the wind stops, and the clouds stop,
When everything grinds down and grains out.
Let mine be a Tuesday, he thought.
                    Let mine be always day-after-tomorrow.

Everything tends toward circumference, it seems—the world,
This life, and no doubt the next,
                    dependence and dear dread,
Even the universe in its spare parts.
                    As for me,
I'm ringed like a tree, stealthily, year by year, moving outward.

Time wears us down and away
Like bootheels, like water on glass,
                                    like footfalls on marble stairs,
Step by slow step until we are edgeless and smoothed out.

And childhood is distant, as distant as the rings of Saturn.

Let loose of my hand, Time, just this once,
And walk behind me along the corridor, the endless one,
That leads to the place I have to go.

There's no erasing the false-front calligraphy of the past.
There's no expunging the way the land lies, and its windfall glare.
I never did get it right.

When the great spider of light unspools her links and chains,
May the past be merciful,
                            the landscape have pity on me —
Forgive me my words, forgive me my utterances.

The water is saying yes and yes in the creekbed.
Clouds have arrived, and last night's moon,
                                    full moon, is a memory.
The wind picks its way through the tight trees
Slowly, as though not to break something.
Marsh snipe on top of the blue spruce.
                                    Nothing in nature says no.

Like tiny ghost dancers, the lupine and Indian paintbrush
Stand still and send back their messages
Through the canyons and black arroyos under the earth.

White horses shade down the deer.
Out of the dank doors in the woods,
                    angels emerge with their bronze foreheads.

And always, beneath the sunlit trees,
The easy breath-pull of moss,
                    gondolas on the black canals
Ferrying back and forth
                    just under the forest floor
The shadows of those who go, and the shadows of those who stay,
Some standing, some sitting down.

Duckweed lies flat on the green water.
The white flags of two deer
                    rattle across the meadow.
Transparent riders appear through the spruce trees and set off for
    the south.
I stand on the near edge of the marsh and watch them disappear.
Like them, I would gladly close my mouth
                    and whisper to no one.

Wind whirls, and dust flies up in eddies.
Flowers rise up and fall,
                    trees buckle, and rise back up and fall.
Summer saddens and grows hot.

Bull snipe cackles in marsh mud.
Hawk corkscrews above the meadow,
                    then dwindles out in the overcast.
Sun back, then swallowed for good.

The world is dirty and dark.
Who thought that words were salvation?
                                    We drift like water.
Whose life is it anyway?

—————

 A misericordia in the wind,
                        summer's symphony
Hustling the silence horizonward,
Black keys from Rimbaud's piano in the Alps struck hard,
Then high tinkles from many white ones.
Then all of it gone to another room of the sky.

Thus do we pass our mornings,
                        or they pass us, waving,
In dark-colored clothes and sad farewells,
The music of melancholy short shrift on their tongues,
Slow sift for the hourglass.
Emptiness fills our fields,
                        new flowers rise from the dead.

The itchings for ultimate form,
                        the braiding of this and that
Together in some abstract design
Is what we're concerned about,
A certain inevitability, a certain redress.
And so we wait for afternoon, and a different weather.

We wait for the consolation of the commonplace,
The belt of light to buckle us in.
We wait for the counterpart,
                        the secretive music
That only we can hear, or we think that only we can hear.

Long afternoons.
                    Long afternoons and long, difficult evenings.

———————

Wind from the northwest,
                    spilling over the edge from Canada.
Big wind. Many steps.
Red bug on the windowpane. This side.
                    Nothing's bothering him
As everything vertical outside
Bends left a lot, then less, then a lot.
                    Red feet, red wings,
A journey beyond the wide world's end, transparent, upside down,
A kind of feckless gesture, like words
We travel back and forth to, one by one,
                    down low and out of the wind.

———————

American midnight, the full moon
Starting its dip behind the mountains.
                    Fluttery shapes,
Fatal as angels in the shadowy corners of the mind,
Flatter the landscape.
Everything seems to coalesce and disintegrate
At once,
        a formal attribute of moonlight, one half
Of which we see, one half of which we maneuver not to see.

No longer interested in
                    the little deaths of fixed forms,
Their bottled formaldehyde,
We follow the narrow road that disappears in the mountains,
We follow the stations of the tongue,

Arc and trailhead,
                    the blaze on the tree.
Look for us soon on the other side
Where the road tumbles down,
                         curving into the invisible city.

———————

Outside, as it does one time each year,
The long body of the Hunter Gracchus sails by on the black water
Between the evergreens.
                         Odor of endlessness. Odor of boat tar.
Dwindling shouts in the twilight. Rustle of aspen leaves.
Woodsmoke. Night birds. Dark linen.

———————

The morning darkens. A wind from the north, winter wind,
Harassing the blue lips
                    of lupine and cornflower.
Like souls of the half-begotten, dead mosses fold their stiff hands.
The trees continue their slow dismemberment and fall.
If there were graves up here
                         they would open at your feet,
The mother appearing in summer and sweet decay.

The natural world, out of whose wounds the supernatural
Rises, and where it longs to return,
Shifts in its socket from time to time
                         and sparks come forth.
These are the cracks, the hyphens of light, the world relinquishes
Briefly, then stanches with human dust.
And that's what's waiting for you in the far meadow,
                    there, where the line's lunar linkup lurks.

———————

The soul starts to talk to itself in the deep sleep of summer.
Under the light-flocked, mismatched spruce boughs,
It begins to know each other.
                              The lonely half looks up at the sky,
The other stares at the dirt.
Who knows what they have to say,
                              their voices like just-strung electric wire,
Constant, unhearable, but live to a single touch.

All guilt and dull ache,
                              we sit in stillness and think of forgotten things.
The stained glare of angel wings,
Radiant Sundays,
Austere, half-opened chambers of the half-opened heart,
Sun-clustered meadow,
The soul surrounding it,
                              a shimmering, speechless lash of light.

———————

Dismantling the damaged bridge,
                              Crash found a water ouzel's nest
Made wholly of moss.
I asked him had he ever seen one, he nodded yes.
I asked him had he ever seen one walk
                              underwater, and he nodded yes.
Over or under, to walk in water is a wondrous thing,
I thought.
         Then thought of Tom, just dead in a foreign land,
And wanted to be an ouzel myself and walk
                              under the North Atlantic
And bring him back, and lay him in the stiff, mossy bed
Forever, above the water,
                              to walk in which is a wondrous thing
In either world, in either station.

Wind lull, and drifting mid-mountain clouds.
Shadows, like huge toads, consume themselves.

Horses lie down

In the mute meadow, birds hold their tongues
As morning prepares itself for the downdraft and broken spoke,
The descent of fiery wheels.

God's chosen walk close to the wall.

———————

Clear-cuts take on a red glow as the dark begins to shut down.
Last pass of the barn swallow,

last lisp of the lingering clouds.

The generator coughs off. Lights out.
Stillness and no echoes, as though a body gathered itself
For a deep journey.
Occasional flicks from the flat and widening stars.
No shank, no shadow.
Footsteps faint through the thickening trees.
And the sound of two hands clapping,

a not unholy music.

———————

Heat-quivering avenues cascade from the clouds,

and half-remembered

Faces roll back, stripped of their foliage,
To haunt their bodies, ghost-gazed and newly peregrine.
Unshod, uncreased, the feet of the recently resurrected
Pass over the dusty passageways

of afternoon, and leave no prints.

Out of the evergreens, one song and a bitter sigh.

How beautiful summer is,
                              unclottable darkness
Seeping across the landscape
Like blood from a hemophiliac.
How strong the heart is to entertain such loveliness.
How stringent the stars are,
                              spreading their welcome across the sky.
Passport stamped, the barrier lifting, how easily one is gathered.

———————

The stars seem like window lights tonight,
                              or streetlights left on to comfort the dead
Unrolling their intergalactic curio maps
This side of midnight.
Their journey is long, and one without amenities.
Mother of Poverty, turn a blind eye on them, let them pass.

Past midnight's the other side,
                              north and south, down-ladder to dawn.
In the slick, cold corridors of the end, it is not our friend.
It's where our echoes reside.
It's what we have to pass through,
                              re-hearing each word we've ever uttered,
Listening one last time to the star-stung sound of our little voices.

———————

The sky is hardening, color of pewter,
                              and ladles its wind
Like watery broth through the pine trees.
Who knows the heart of another's heart?
Our lives are the length of a struck match,
And our days are sure to end in a dark confusion.

———————

Where the deer trail sinks down in the August shade of the pine trees,
There, on the other side of the creek,
Sapsucker off-rhythm drums

                    in the lodgepole and tamarack.
A knocking, as though he would enter,
Or exit, something
Dimmed and wind-whipped, riddled with wormways.

The blue flowers of summer
Turn toward us on their stiff stalks their sinister faces.
Something red dies out in us,

                    and closes its eyelids.
I want to become a horseman, a Mongol rider.
I want to become the black of the sapsucker's wing,
An absence of all color,

               a feathery geography.

———————

Chortle, and stuttering half-lilt, of an unknown bird.
They are burying Tom in West Virginia in a couple of days.
Butterfly yo-yoing back and forth above the short flowers.

White horse and mule and fjord horse

                    at grass in the glistering field.
They are burying Tom in West Virginia on Monday next.
Hum and hiccup of generator, hum of the creek.

Black dog and golden dog at large in the meadow marsh.
They are burying Tom in West Virginia, and that is that,
Butterfly back at the dandelion,

              as cosmopolitan as the weed.

———————

Like memory, night is kind to us,
Erasing idle details.
                    Circumference, for instance. Or linearity.
Astronomy starts to make some sense, and verticality.
Like sediment, inch after inch, we rise toward the stars.

———————

The formalist implications of the afterlife
Seem to reveal, so far,
                    one star and a black voyage
To rediscover our names,
Our real names, imperishably inscribed in the registry of light,
From which all letters befall.

And that suits me for the time being,
Afternoon's alphabet beginning to firm up in the field,
Such radiant lettering.
If one only knew the name he was practicing for,
It would be easily there.

The world is a magic book, and we its sentences.
We read it and read ourselves.
                    We close it and turn the page down
And never come back,
Returned to what we once were before we became what we are.
This is the tale the world tells, this is the way it ends.

BUFFALO YOGA CODAS

Buffalo Yoga Coda I

Low deck, Montana sky
                    color of cold Confederate uniforms,
High water in all the creeks, trees down
From wind and wet, beginning of June,
Snow yesterday, hard rain and hard frost, three bags full,
Whitecaps and white river, welcome back,
The tamaracks whisper and the lodgepole and the sough.

I slip the word in my shirt pocket: Time.
To warm it, to keep it dark, to keep it back from Forever.
I fold it in half and hold it there.
Like the cicada, however, it leaves its body and goes about its business,
Slick shell, such beautiful wings,
A corpse to reckon with.
                    Memento mori, perhaps.

———————

That which we leave unspoken is like the hail from last night's storm
Still clustered and white
                    in the shadowy tall grass, as yet unreached by the sun.
Like unuttered words, they disappear
One by one in the light,
                    crystal and golden for an instant, then nothing at all.
Like everything else not done or not chosen.
Like all that's liquid and overlooked,
                              what we don't give, what we don't take.

———————

Bullbat's back,
                high up and almost unseeable in the morning's glare,

Swallows a hyperkinetic singsong down below.
I daydream about a pierced, medieval vision,

                                         a suppuration of wounds,

A spurting of blood,
One ladle, two quick and endless gulps.
St. Catherine of Siena, drink something from me.

Like the patch of late snow each one of us has left in his heart
Hoarding some hurt or other,

                         some wind chime of vague consequence,
The world has a caked and cold spot for the self-deceived,
No matter how much they glitter and spark in the sleeved sunfall.
Theirs is the dark inheritance of the doubly dead.
For them the snuffed flame, the Fifteenth Station of the Cross.

———————

Like intercessionary prayers to Purgatory,
Our little whines and our simperings
Flutter into the weather.
No wonder no answer is all we ever get, no wonder.

The purple violets are just back in the long grass.
You don't hear a peep from them,
Intent, as they are, on doing whatever it is they're here to do.
Look how low they lie in the wind,

                         how pursed their lips are.

———————

In the high house of oblivion, there are many windows.
Through one of them, a light like the light
Now sliding across the meadow slides,

                            burst and perpetual.
One knows it from old frames of celluloid, exposed some,
That scorch like a wood flame, a hard light

That does not illuminate, but outlines and silhouettes.
Inside its panes the snow falls,
$\qquad\qquad\qquad$ defining and flame-colored snow.
Through all the rest, no light shines,
Silence breeds and recalibrates, no waters whiffle, no wind.

———————

Night fog, denser and denser.
Above it, an endlessness,
$\qquad\qquad\qquad$ flight path for the newly received.
Or so they want to believe, their poor hands like poor flags in the
$\qquad$ distance.
Down here, however, it's difficult.
Down here, it's a different story.
$\qquad\qquad\qquad$ This world, no thought of the other.

We'd like the fog to drift and rise, but it hugs the ground.
Like words we meant to say, but didn't.
We'd like to tell the departed to come back,
$\qquad\qquad\qquad$ to say we're sorry for what we didn't say.
If, in fact, they're up there.
If, in fact, they're not still here,
$\qquad\qquad\qquad$ still hugging the ground like the fog, like us.

———————

I think I'll lie down just here for a while,
$\qquad\qquad\qquad$ the sun on my cheek,
The wind like grass stems across my face,
And listen to what the world says,
$\qquad\qquad\qquad$ the luminous, transubstantiated world,
That holds me like nothing in its look.

Buffalo Yoga Coda II

If, as Kafka says, the hunting dogs,
At play in the stone courtyard,
Will catch the hare no matter,
                                    regardless of how it may be flying
Already now through the dark forest,
Then it must stay itself with just these trees,
                                    and their bright passage,
Those marks and punctuations before the sentence ends,
Before, in short, and black as a bible,
                                    the period closes in.

If, on the other hand, the hunting dogs,
                                    now at play
In the stone courtyard,
Never arrive, the story becomes less classical.
And the hare, however fast,
                                    will always be slow enough
To outlast the ending, which presupposes the source
Of story and story line,
Which cannot be doubted, and so the period snaps in place.

And thus one parable becomes another, the sun,
As it must, continues its chords and variations,
The waters lisp in the speckled woods,
The deer put their tentative feet,
                                    one forward, one back,
On the dead pine needles and dead grass,
Then turn like Nijinsky out of the sunlight and up the hill.
When Tolstoy met Chekhov, Chekhov says,
                                    they spoke of immortality, what else.

Outside the outhouse doorframe, dewbows, a spatter of
Word-crystals, little eternities,
                                    each one of them,
Syllable, syllable, one handful of sleep, then two.

The long body of the Hunter Gracchus,
                                    needle on Kafka's compass,
Slides through the upper meadow out of the south-southwest
As it does each year,
Ceaselessly circumnavigating
Our lives,
        always true north, the black river just inches above the ground,
Time's sluice and time's undertow,
On its way to Mt. Caribou, and on toward the northern lights.

The dove finds no olive leaf,
                                    so it slips back to the darkness inside the ark,
He wrote toward the end of his short, pain-dominant life.
And who would say otherwise?
There was a bird in the room, he wrote,
Each of his limbs as tired as a whole human being.
Whoever heard of a dying man drinking?
                                    he asked, unable to do so himself.
And who would ask otherwise?

Late spring in the upper northwest,
                                    first day of summer and the lilac just out,
Pale purple and dark purple
Over the white of the propane tank in back of the cabin.
The lilac is wonderful, isn't it? he wrote once,
Even when dying it drinks,
                                    like a fish you might say.

Pale purple and dark purple,
And green of the underleaf, and green of the meadow.

I take down the thin book of All I Will Ever Know,
And find them, the one entry,
Three tiny words, three poised and tail-lifted scorpions.

Inadequate to the demands
                          imagination has settled upon me,
I listen to what the landscape says,
And all that it fails to say, and what the clouds say, and the light,
Inveterate stutterer.
                    Not much this morning, it turns out,
Odor of lilac like a south wind
Suddenly through the open window, swallow twaddle
Inelegant under the raw eaves.

Kafka appears in a splotch of sunlight
                                  beyond the creek's course,
Ready, it seems, to step off the *via dolorosa* he's walked through the
      dark forest.
I offer him bread, I offer him wine and soft cheese,
But he stands there, hands in his pockets,
Shaking his head no, shaking his head,
                                  unable, still,
To speak or eat or to drink.
Then raises his right hand and points to the lilacs,
                          smiles, and changes back into sunlight.

Buffalo Yoga Coda III

Late morning on the cusp of the world,
Clouds beginning to burble and build
                                    across the southern skyline,
Susurration of waters,
Sunlight settling like a giant bird
Soundlessly over the meadow,
                            feathery touches at the edges of things.

The raven is yakking and looking for somewhere to land,
                                    the restless raven,
Begetter of aches and many wounds,
Malicious informant, *boia* of the airy blue.
One tree's not good enough;
                            he tries another and then a third.
He's got his bright eye on me.

Under the low hum of the sweet bees,
Under the hair-heavy hoof of the warrior ant,
Under the towering shadows he must go through,
                                    and surface from,
Under the beetle's breast and the grub's,
The future is setting its table,
                        its cutlery dark, its mirrors anxious and blank.

———————

Can sunlight rustle across the skin?
Can dew fall upon the eye?
Can lamentations of the unborn grieve in the wind?
Can alien constellations comfort the sore children?

Can the hands of the dead rise?
Can God untwist all that he's twisted?
Can horizons steal our breath?
Can we take back the borrowed dust we've given away?
Can the right word ring, O my, forever in the ear?
Can a selfish song be its own praise?

These are the simulacra of our days,
                              the June clouds
Like Navajo rugs on heaven's floor,
Grey-black in the underwarp,
Dullness of distance in the shadowless corridors
Down through the forest,
                              lilacs deglazed and past repair,
Pine squirrels riding the grub line from thicket to windowsill
     and back.

Humdrum and extracurricular,
                         the waters turn from our touch, the grass yields,
And all the spidery elegance of afternoon
Lays down its weary body,
Legs tucked and dimmed some,
                              unbidden and warm at our feet.
It's somebody's birthday, the 27th of June.
Sitting outside on the new-laid steps, I sharpen my pencil

To rig up his elegy,
Which this is, at least in part, and mine as well, I guess,
If the road he takes to return here
Is Koo Koo Boyd or Solo Joe,
                              French Garver or Basin Creek;
And if, in the Indian paintbrush sundown, the sound
He hears is the bullbat or summer snipe,
                              then this is for both of us.

A fine rain and a fine mist,

                        return of the great blue heron
To Porcupine and its upper reaches, above the creek bridge.
How beautiful summer is,

                    with all its creatures and all its weather,
Sunblade for just a second, then back in its scabbard of clouds,
Robins and rain continuing to pierce and pick at the earth,
Great blue at the top of the last larch,

                            eye ready for his turn.

Last legs of the lilac, but here come the lupine and bear grass,
The paintbrush and yarrow stalks.
Black ants work the underground,

                freelancing among the stones and clay lumps,
Their slighter cousins hard and orderly at the weeds.

Two whitetail does, flags up, at romp in the near meadow,
One snipe in a sexual dive and collapse

                      just there, in the marsh slough,
Moose at the salt block,
East-inching shadows like black tongues licking themselves up.

I think I'll lie down just here for a while,

                      the sun on my cheek,
The wind like grass stems across my face,
And listen to what the world says,

                    the luminous, transubstantiated world,
That holds me like nothing in its look.

SNAKE EYES

The Gospel According to St. Someone

Reflected radiance, moon envy, we hang outside
Ourselves like bats,
                    clothed in our flash dreams.
Sunset soaks down to the last leaves of the autumn trees.
Under our heads, the world is a long drop and an ache.
Above us, the sky forks,
                    great road to the left, great road to the right.

Someone will come and walk on his hands
                              through the dry grass to the altar.
Someone will take the wafer, someone will take the wine
And walk back through the gravestones.
Succor us, someone,
Let us drink from your mouth and let us eat from your tongue.

Eternal penny, counterfeit truth, score us and pay us off.
Buried November, read us our rites.
Salvation, worry our sins.
Awake, we all share the same world,
                              asleep, we're each in our own.
Lay me down, Lord, let me sleep.

Homage to Mark Rothko

I tried their ways for a little while,
But wasn't at ease with them, they

not bringing me to the revealed.
Still, I kept on praising them.
I cast my body upon the earth.
I cast my body upon the waters,

and kept on praising them all.
The glories refused to shelter me,
Nothing explained, nothing brought to bear.
I tried their ways for a little while,

but nothing was ever revealed.

————————

We enter the fields of memory and devotion.
Allow me, as Paul Celan says,

to thank you from there—
Landscape, this world, this poor earth
Under the sun, holding nothing back,
This almost-nature that goes from light to light, that melts
The gold coin between our teeth,
That raises, like water, the shadow of the wound

up to our necks.
Allow me to thank you from all the language there is in that.

Early December, autumn's ragtag and cockamamie end.
Next door, Doctor Dave's got his pickup truck at the raked leaf
        pile,
Bird feeders float like flying saucers

suddenly through the trees,

Plaster Madonna and wood-cut edge of the Blue Ridge
Zoomed in by the bare branches.
Turkey buzzards and crows
                              drifting like lint on the Piedmont sky,
December, ragtag and gypsy day.
Allow me to thank you from all that's missing in all of that.

Form cannot deconstruct or be annihilated, you said.
The communion of saints,
                              desire and its aftermath,
Chalice and chasuble, bread and wine—
Just sonar of purification, imprints,
                                        pretty tomfoolery.
Whatever *it* is, it's beyond all this, you said.
                              And painting and language and music.
Stars are the first pages, you said, in The Book of Unknowing.
Behind them are all the rest.
Form is eternal and exists unwreckable, past repair, you said.

                    ————————

In the light that shines without shadow,
                                        our hiding place.
Comfort metastasizes.
Wintering in. Wintering in to distance and wordlessness.
Comfort blackens the X rays.
                              Echoes, deep subtractions.
Wretched the body dependent upon the body.
Wretched the flesh and the soul therein.
I tried to give form to the formless,
                              and speech to the unspeakable.
To the light that shines without shadow, I gave myself.

Portrait of the Artist in a
Prospect of Stone

Here is a photograph of George Mancini and me
On Hydra, the 23 March, 1961.
We're out on the breakwater.
                              An American girl named Merle
Is next to George, who's reading a newspaper. Eric,
An Englishman, and Le Grand Danois
Are next to her.
  Feta, the dog, stands foursquare and panting in the cold Aegean sun.
I'm at the far end, looking at George,
Sunglasses, white socks, and desert boots,
                                        Lieutenant's last morning.
Axel Jensen, outside the frame's edge, is up the rock-warped hill.
He's writing a first novel.
About his days with the Tuareg nomads in Algeria.
Or maybe Morocco. It's hard to remember everything.

Do I remember the would-be American novelist
Rewriting Proust for the middle west?
                              Just out of the Air Force,
He'd spent a year on the island, sleeping with some musician's wife,
Also, it turned out, American.
I, of course, loved all of this.
What else was a 25-year-old,
                              Armied and under wraps for years,
Supposed to fall in love with?
Back in Verona, that army was looking for me.
Security violation, a missing classified document.

Ciccolella, our G-2, would tell my colonel,
                    "We don't come down on our own."
Meanwhile, I sat in the almost-April Greek sunshine
Romancing expatriates,
                    hoping for my turn to become like one of them.

Mancini remembers less than I.
                    Or says he does,
Patmos just to the east, where much was revealed to John.
The winds out of Asia ride hard herd on the waves.
Narrative's narrative is seldom as slick as it purports to be,
We know, but what is this red paint print above our heads?
Ricordo di Roma, thumb smear
                    by Mary who did the oil painting
There on the wall from the photograph on Via del Babuino.
You're blocking my view of God,
                    Tom said to his ex-intended,
Camel caravans moving like Bergman across the sand dunes,
Gods bright in the bright Aegean air.
Axel dreams of his Berber robes,
                    I dream, in my white socks, of permanent leave,
And Greece, a sleep and forget-me-not, is long, and has no dreams.

Listen, memory's got a hard heart and a soft head.
Whatever light the eye sees, the heart says dark, dark, dark.
Nothing is ever lost, I once said.
                    That was untrue,
I know now, the past a hiding place
Beyond recall or recovery, no matter our wants or our diligence.
Whatever is gone is gone,
Settling like sand dollars under memory's eyelid,
Down to the darkness where nothing stirs,
                              nothing except the heart,
That eyeless fish, drifting on slow, invisible currents

Beneath a blue hopscotch of islands where,

                              up above,
Somebody young and undiminished assembles a few friends
Along a breakwater in the sun.

                    Then one of them takes a camera out.

Rosso Venexiano

And here is a photograph of me taking a photograph
Of Holly and me. In 1969, I think,
In Venice,
               Timothy Hennessey's wretched painting
Behind us, the ornate Venetian mirror throwing us back
Spotted, rejuvenate, shelved in two.

And that's not half bad, I'd say,
Chihuly downstairs, and Luke Hodgkin, *acqua alta*
Finally out the door,
               the schifo from the trattoria
Flushed through the ground floor hallway's side rooms,
The lettuce flats and cardboard wine boxes
                           sucked back toward Malamocco.

End of March, thirty-three years ago.
Across the water, in S. Sebastiano, the Veronesi
Are arc-lit and scaffolded,
The Phantom Turk, square-rigged ghost ship,
                         still moored on the Grand Canal
In front of Palazzo Guggenheim.

Or so we imagined it,
               Corvo at large on the damp streets,
Pound on his daily constitutional, as I've said before,
Exhuming the Zattere and Innocenti,
Fluttering candlelike guttering light
At night in the windows high up in Palazzo Barbaro.

Our altered and unreal lives.

How silly it all was, how delicious,
Palazzo this and Palazzo that,
Guardi and Canaletto from every bridge and opening,
The gold-domed Dogana a harsh relief in the winter sun.
Nobody sat on the steps that year,

not I, not anyone.

What else is bereft in the camera's lens, or the mirror's eye?
People, of course, and the future; Campo S. Polo:
Sabo, co fa scuro, Gran Balo Macabro, the poster announced.
Lord, the detritus.

Write, the voice said. *For whom?* came the response.
For the dead whom thou didst love, came the instant reply.

And will they read me?
Aye, for they return as posterity, the voice answered one last time.
Red of Titian's *Assumption*, red of the Doge's fingernail,
Blood red of the *Serenissima*,
Lagoon light, sunset and cloud blaze,

red of the Cardinal entourage.

Words Are the Diminution of All Things

The brief secrets are still here,
                        and the light has come back.
The word *remember* touches my hand,
But I shake it off and watch the turkey buzzards bank and wheel
Against the occluded sky.
All of the little names sink down,
                        weighted with what is invisible,
But no one will utter them, no one will smooth their rumpled hair.

There isn't much time, in any case.
There isn't much left to talk about
                    as the year deflates.
There isn't a lot to add.
Road-worn, December-colored, they cluster like unattractive angels
Wherever a thing appears,
Crisp and unspoken, unspeakable
                      in their mute and glittering garb.

All afternoon the clouds have been sliding toward us
                        out of the Blue Ridge.
All afternoon the leaves have scuttled
Across the sidewalk and driveway, clicking their clattery claws.
And now the evening is over us,
Small slices of silence
                  running under a dark rain,
Wrapped in a larger.

45

Arrivederci Kingsport

It's all Interstate anymore,
                              the sedge fields Ted Glynn and I
Would shoot doves on. Or underwater.
The Country Music Highway, out of the hollers and backwash
Of southeastern Kentucky, old U.S. 23,
Has carried the boys to a different demarcation,
Their voices like field mice in the 21st-century wind.

Goodbye to that stuff,
The late '40s and early '50s and adolescence,
Dolores Urquiza and Clara Hall
                              —memory's music just out of tune—
Drifting in their 7th-grade frocks across the Civic Auditorium floor.
Goodbye to Sundays, and band practice,
                              the backseats of cars,
Goodbye to WKPT and everybody's song.

Jesus, it's all still a fist of mist
That keeps on cleaning my clock,
                              tick-tock, my youth, tick-tock, my youth,
Everything going away again and again toward the light.
Who will remember Christina Marsh and Bobby Step,
                              now that I'm gone?
Who will remember the frog famine,
Now that the nameless roads
                              have carried us all from town?

Midsummer in 1951,
                    the censer gone,
The call-and-response both gone, how far away is that?

A life unremarkable, but one which was remarked,
It turns out. Without consolation, it seemed,
                              adolescence,
The summer seeped to its end,
The sweet smoke of the past like bandages
                              on all our imagined wounds.

And once upon a time, in the long afternoons of autumn,
The boys and girls would lay them down
                              in the bitter weeds
And watch the hidden meanderings
Of stars in their luminous disguise,
                    that ill-invested blue.
Is there reprieve for this act?
Is there reprieve for such regard?
                    Not in this life, and not in the next.

Well, yes, but beside the point.
And what is the point?
                    The point is the drawn-out landfall
From Chestnut Ridge to Moccasin Gap.
The point is U.S. 11W disappearing
In front of us and behind our backs,
                              the winter winds
And the clouds that dog our footsteps, out west and back east.

And so the dance continues,
Boots Duke and Jackie Imray,
                    Bevo and Kay Churchill,
Jim Churchill and Nancy Sims,
Name after name dropping into the dark waters of day-before-yesterday.
Champe Bachelder and Karen Beall,
                              Bill Ring and Sarah Lou,
Slow dance, the music coming up again.

Goodnight, sweetheart, well, it's time to go.
Ta-ta-ta-ta-tum, Goodnight, sweetheart, well, it's time to go,
                              the soft-aired, Tennessee night
Gathers its children in its cupped hands.
Time has its covenant, and who's to say that it is unjust.
We make our sad arrangements.
                         The sky clears, the sun sets.
No matter the words, we never forget our own song.

January II

A cold draft blows steadily from a crack in the window jamb.
It's good for the soul.
For some reason, I think of monuments in the high desert,
                                        and what dissembles them.

We're all born with a one-way ticket, of course,
Thus do we take our deaths up on our shoulders and walk and
        walk,
Trying to get back.

We'd like to move as the water moves.
We'd like to cover the earth
                                the way the wind covers the earth.
We'd like to burn our way there, like fire.

It's not in the cards.
Uncertainty harbors us like winter mist—
                                the further we go, the deeper it gets.
Sundown now, and wind from the northwest.

The month is abandoned.
                                Volvos go wandering to and fro
Like lost polar bears. The landscape is simple and brown.
The future's behind us, panting, lolling its black tongue.

Dio Ed Io

There is a heaviness between us,
Nameless, raised from the void, that counts out the sprung hours.
What ash has it come to purify?
What disappearance, like water, does it lift up to the clouds?

God of my fathers, but not of mine,
You are a part, it is said, an afterthought, a scattered one.
There is a disappearance between us as heavy as dirt.
What figure of earth and clay would it have me become?

Sunday again, January thaw back big-time.
The knock-kneed, overweight boys and girls
Sit on the sun-warmed concrete sidewalk outside the pharmacy
Smoking their dun-filtered cigarettes.

Nothing is bothering them—and their nicotine dreams—
This afternoon. Everything's weightless,
As insubstantial as smoke.
Nothing is disappearing in their world. Arrival is all.

There is a picture of Yves Klein leaping out of a window
Above a cobblestone Paris street.
A man on a bicycle pedals away toward the distance.
One of them's you, the other is me.

Cut out of the doctored photograph, however, the mesh net
Right under the swan-diving body.
Cut out of another print, the black-capped, ever-distancing cyclist, as
     well as the mesh net.
Hmmm . . . And there you have it, two-fingered sleight-of-hand man.

One loses one's center in the air, trying to stay afloat,
Doesn't one? Snowfalling metaphors.
Unbidden tears, the off-size of small apples. Unshed.
And unshedable.

Such heaviness. The world has come and lies between us.
Such distance. Ungraspable.
Ash and its disappearance —
Unbearable absence of being,
                              Tonto, then taken back.

Nostalgia III

Sun-sliding morning. The doors of the world stand open,
The one up and the one down.
        Twice-blessed by their golden handles,
We try them both, but they don't open, not yet, they don't open.

Wind from the west as usual,
       harp-limbs of bare trees
In southwest corner of things.
The music of memory has its own pitch,
         which not everyone hears.

Cloud-gondolas floating in with the east-moving wind-waters,
Black-hulled and gilt-edged,
      white on white up above, smooth pole.
Later, the sunset, flamingo, great bird of passage.

Dry autumn and dry winter, dry spring.
The nights drift over us,
      spun toward the iron Atlantic.
Memory's mantras hum like electric lights in their slow flow.

Bits, and small bits, and pieces of things.
Memory has its own affections,
       bleak, unappointed rounds,
High beams in the dark driveway, no one behind the wheel.

In Praise of Thomas Chatterton

Humdrum of helicopter dwindling off to the west,
Full moon in a night or two.
Why do I think of Chatterton, *the marvellous boy,*
Just seventeen and under the hill over two hundred years ago?
Is it the bulge of the moon?
                Is it the double consonant of wind and the weather?

Both Keats and Wordsworth thought well of him.
The purest English, I think, is Chatterton's, Keats wrote
In a letter to George in Louisville, Kentucky.
Wordsworth referred to him as *the sleepless soul that perished in his
      pride,*
Inventing his own vocabulary, dead by his own hand.

I remember seeing a picture once, an inked engraving, I think,
Of Chatterton as a suicide,
Sprawled on his bed, gargoyles and fanged, feathery creatures
Circling above him.
Outside the window, a moon like this one.
              God rest him, *and happie bee hys dolle.*

Charles Wright and the 940 Locust Avenue Heraclitean Rhythm Band

The declination of desire
                    is greatly to be desired.
Likewise cessation of laud and lisp.
Out of the west window, lights like the lights of floating seabirds.
Tides of darkness rock them among the trees, back and forth,
Forth and back,
Desire, at last, a remembered landscape,
                              and never the same hurt twice.

A long steel rail and a short crosstie,
The song continues,
                    the lights now settling in the trees,
The darkness rocking them back and forth, pulling them in.
They're never the same lights twice, although
—Like memory in the present tense—
That train, the Streamlined Cannonball,
                    keeps bringing me back to the same flame.

I'm on my way back home,
                    the darkness gathers them in.
A door opens, a door closes, all doors are holy,
It's traced in the book's margin, the lights open and close,
Reflected stars in the oak trees
                    perched in their branches.
Like star birds of brief passage.
Light is a doorway, darling, I'm on my way back home.

Desire and landscape,
              dry hour after rain, drifting us deep into the evening.
When was it desire devolved into memory, when
Did the X become the Y?
The stars have opened their bottomless throats, and started their
        songs.
They are not singing to us,
It turns out, they are not singing their watery songs to us.

And do we care about that? Of course.
We are the travellers down below,
                              without sisters, without brothers.
Inside us the earth is turned over into a new language.
Inside us the seeds
              oboe their inventory, their shadow music.
And never the same song twice,
And never the same life twice, who knows which one is the better?

Saturday Afternoon

The sadness of sunlight lies like fine dust on the evergreens.
Even the wind can't move it,
The wind that settles across the afternoon like a luck-hungry bird,
Reshuffling its feathers from time to time,
                                    and cricking its claws.
The slow sleep and sad shine of sunlight.

Shadows are clumsy and crude, their eggs few,
And dragonflies, like lumescent Ohio Blue Tip matchsticks,
Puzzle the part-opened iris stalks,
                                    hovering and stiff.
New flies frenetic against the glass,
Woodpeckers at their clocks,
                        the horses ablaze in the grained light.

Although the lilac is long dead, the bees still seek its entrance.
In vain, the chilled and resurgent bees.
It's not so much the lilac they want
As subtraction of lilac,
                            some sumptuous, idyllic door
Unlatching to them its inner and sumptuous rooms.

The season, however, outlegs them,
Unanswerable in its instruments
                            and its empty cells.
And bees must follow it willy-nilly, and lockstep,
Right down the air, where the world reloads
                                    and offers up
Its lesser mansions, its smaller rooms.

This is no metaphor, this is the way it just is,
Creaking of wheels endemic under the earth,

                                    slick pistil and piston,
Pulleys raising the platforms up, and pulling them down.
We walk on the roofs of great houses,

                                    some of them quick, some not,
All of them turning like a river, all of them ours.

Wednesday Morning

There is a stillness across the morning,
                              sudden absence of something,
Horses escaped, birds mum, the wind that has stopped blowing.
The strict vocabulary of the dead has a word for it,
This stillness, that still escapes us
                        like breath, like grain through our fingers.
But like the birds, they are mum.
And like the horses, and like the wind,
                              they stay that way.

For the time being, at least.
At least until the dead come back, and both the horses do, and the
        birds.
At least until the morning recovers her balance,
And rises,
            up from her one elbow,
Her blue hand on her blue hip,
And parcels herself into a luminance, and sings.

Until then, we mull it and mark its dark erasures.
The trees go on holding their arms out.
The sunlight, with its ship's code
Stealthily signalling from water to willow leaf and back,
Explains it once and for all,
But we can see nothing, or take in nothing, it is so still.

There is a stillness in us, too,
                              a different stillness, one like a light's flash
From one end of a grain of sand to the other end,

Tiny, that longs to impose itself on our vague solitude,
And on our incumbent lives.
Essential stillness at the center of things,

                              the stillness of stones,
Stillness of all that we do not do, that we are not.

It's not, as I say, the same story,
Pointillist array of yellowweed unmovable
In the far meadow.

                    But look,
A breath from the blue lady, a bend in the long-legged grass,
The stillness beginning to grow small,

                              and smaller still,
Until it is overgrown, and hidden, as ours is.

Homage to Giorgio Morandi

You, of all the masters, have been the secret sharer
Of what's most important,
                              exclusion,
Until the form is given us out of what has been given,
And never imposed upon,
Scrape and erase, scrape and erase
                              until the object comes clear.

I well remember the time I didn't visit you
In Bologna, 1964,
                    the year you died.
Bob Koffler and Wolf Kahn went, Mary and all the rest of us
Remaining in Rome. What a mistake.
The next thing we heard was your *coccodrillo* in the *Daily American*.

And now you've become iconic, as only is right,
Grizzano and atelier,
                          permanent as a pair of finger rings
On your worldwide hands.
The farther out of the picture you go, the greater it grows.
The farther out of our lives you go, *la stessa storia*.

And now you have become an eternal occasion.
The less in view, the more your presence
Surrounds us,
                  and concentrates our tick-tock attention.
How proper it is we see you most where you are not,
Among your objects.
                    This bottle, for instance, this vase.

Bologna made you and Bologna undid you in the scheme of things.
It never mattered to you.
How little we knew about your life,

                              how little we knew about anything,
The Roman nights so florid and opposite of all that you stood for.
We bathed in our own dark waters,

                    you dabbled your brush in yours.

The would-be artist's credo—
He keeps to himself

                    and doesn't play well with others—
Found short shrift on your star chart.
Still, no serious time for anything but your work,
You looked as hard as anyone ever looked,

                              then left it out.

Little Apocalypse

The butterfly's out on noon patrol,
                              dragoning down to the rapt flower heads.
The ground shudders beneath the ant's hoof.
Under cover of sunlight, the dung beetle bores through his summer
        dreams.
High up, in another world,
                        the clouds assemble and mumble their messages.
Sedate, avaricious life,

The earthworm huddled in darkness,
                                  the robin, great warrior, above,
Reworking across the shattered graves of his fathers.
The grass, in its green time, bows to whatever moves it.
Afternoon's ready to shove its spade
                                  deep in the dirt,
Coffins and sugar bones awash in the sudden sun.

Inside the basements of the world,
                                the clear-out's begun,
Lightning around the thunder-throat of the underearth,
A drop of fire and a drop of fire,
Bright bandages of fog
                        starting to comfort the aftermath.
Then, from the black horizon, four horses heave up, flash on their
        faces.

Snake Eyes

The afternoon clouds are like a Xerox of the morning clouds,
An indecipherable transcript,
                                    ill-litanied, ill-limned.

There is no consolation, it seems, there's only light.
Right there, beyond our dark spot.

Imagination is merely the door.
                                    All we can do is knock hard
And hope that something will open it.

Around the corners of the known world,
                                    blue stanzas link
The lines of the first great poem, there is no second.

Idleness anchors us.
                                    Nothing accomplished, nothing retrieved,
We're posed like water striders above the secondhand stars.

We have a taste for the untasteable,
                                    the radiant root of things,
The unimaginary part of what is unimaginable.

We wait between goodbye and hello,
                                    an ounce of absence, an ounce of regret,
Standing on one foot, whistling a half-remembered tune.

Mystical twos and mojo, God sockets,
                                    clouds roll across the sky,
Letting the light come down on some, taking it back from others.

My Own Little Civil War

I come from the only county in Tennessee that did not secede
Throughout the entire Civil War,
                                    Sullivan County,
Rock-ribbed, recalcitrant, Appalachian cornerstone.
My kinfolk were otherwise,
Arkansans and Mississippians,
                                    Virginians and Tarheels.
Still, I was born just a half mile from Shiloh churchyard,
And had a relative, the family story goes, who served there,
Confederate quartermaster,
                                    who took the occasion, that first day,
To liberate many bills
From Union coffers as the Johnnys swept through to the river,
And never replaced them when the Bluebellies swept back
And through the following afternoon.

My great-grandfather Wright left VMI to join up
With Lee and the Army of Northern Virginia
Somewhere near Richmond,
                            and ended up,
Lucky lad, a staff officer in the general's command.
Who knows how many letters that took?
After the war he went back to Lexington, with Lee,
The general to Washington College and immortality,
Capt. Wright at the far end of town,
                                    still marching away the lost cause.
Marse Robert has his horse and white tomb
Under the oak trees.
My great-grandfather has his name in a long thin line

Of others who were Captains of the Corps of Cadets,
                                        too little, boys, too late.

My great-grandfather Penzel, four years in the country,
Saddled up in 1861 in Little Rock
With the Capital City Guards
                              and struck out for Tennessee.
His name is last on the list, carved in print on an obelisk,
In front of a civic building somewhere near downtown.
Like just about everyone else, he finished the war as a captain,
Enduring the raw campaigns
                              of southeast Tennessee,
Chickamauga, two years in Rock Island prison, deep
Wounds in his mouth and elsewhere,
Then back, like all the others, into the thick of it.
A long way for a country boy,
                              slaveless, and no stake in it,
From the green hills of Bohemia.

There are letters from Isaac Wright,
                              Bladen County, North Carolina,
1856,
To his son near Lafayette Courthouse, Red River, Arkansas,
A dozen or so, I cannot decipher.
                              Political
And familial, about President Franklin Pierce,
Wishing that John C. Calhoun
                              were still alive and president
Instead, and the Constitutional rights of the South
Established with greater force,
                              and greater clarity.
"I fear that we shall yet have difficulties with our Northern Brethren."
And then the price of negroes,

Nearby farms, the fear of high water,
                    the price of cotton, always the price of cotton.
Then "love to Elizabeth, my son, and you and the children."

All this from the documents
                    left by my great-aunt Marcella,
A folder that also holds,
Inexplicably, my grandmother's marriage license
And one short sketch, so titled, of the Fulton and Nowland families.
So much for all that . . .
                    However, wrapped in wax paper,
Among the letters, is another small envelope
Containing a lock, so called,
                    of Robert E. Lee's hair,
Sent by him to the wife of the lucky lad from VMI . . .
That's it, my own little Civil War—
                    a lock of hair,
A dozen unreadable letters,
An obit or two,
And half the weight and half-life
                    of a half-healed and hurting world.

La Dolceamara Vita

Autumn is over. The winter rains
Have settled like feathers from wild geese
                                deep in the trees.

I start my afternoon rote walk, the wet-step and weekend one,
Up Locust Avenue and back down.

The cold-eaten, sap-sunken gold of the maple leaves
Takes in the light and grows big,

The church chimes like empty villages,
                                ruin-riddled, far away,
Where nobody goes.

The dogwood is redder now than summer's chokecherry,
Sunset sheen like old wax on the steps into the sky,

Rainwater gone, drifting under the streets while nobody notices.
I reach the hospital and turn back.

Behind me, day darkens, in front of me darker still.
If I had it all to do over again, I'd pull the light

Toward me and start to gleam,
                                and then not gleam, the way the leaves do,
The dying leaves, and the cold flowers.

Sun-Saddled, Coke-Copping, Bad-Boozing Blues

Front porch of the first cabin, with Luke.
July, most likely, and damp, both of us wearing rubber boots.
Just out of the photograph, beyond the toe of my left foot,
The railing where Tim and I, one afternoon,

                              carved our poor initials
While working on verses for his song, "Stockman's Bar Again, Boys."
Both song and singer are gone now, and the railing too.

We all sang in the chorus

                        back in L.A., in the recording studio,
Holly and I and Bill Myers and Kelly and Johnny Rubinstein.
Such joyful music, so long ago,

                      before the coke crash and the whiskey blows.
Sun-soured Montana daydreams,
Los Angeles and its dark snood so soft on the neck.
Lie still I'm working on it lie still.

Billy Mitchell's just come by, somebody stole his tools,
Leland Driggs has shot an elk and broke the county's rules.
Sweet Dan Kelly's on his Cat, watch out and back away,
Snuffy Bruns is feeding squirrels and Crash is bucking hay.
Big John Phelan's got outside a half a fifth of gin,
We've all gone and gotten drunk in Stockman's Bar again.

Dead frequency, Slick, over and out.
It's mostly a matter of what kind of noise you make.
American Hot Wax, for instance, and "Stand by Your Man" —

                  George Jones, type-casting for sure.

And music, always music—keyboard and guitar, violin,
Anything with a string.
                    Your band was called Fun Zone, you up front,
Poncher on drums, Wolfie on bass, and Johnny R. at the piano.

And others. Until the lights went out.
                    Renaissance boy,
With coke up your nose and marijuana in your eye,
We loved you the best we could, but nobody loved you enough.
Except Miss Whiskey.
You roll in your sweet baby's arms now, as once you said you
     would,
And lay your body down,
                    in your meadow, in the mountains, all alone.

                    —*Tim McIntire (1944–1986)*

Sinology

This floating life, no anchor at either end, just white
Back here and white there.
An old memory of my mother when she was young
Ruffs like an egret and settles back.

———————

The winds peruse us, the clouds roll and offer their offices.
We try to avoid all this, and sidestep our itches.
Like winter landscapes,
We huddle inside our own signatures,

                         not yet alive, not yet dead.

———————

The twilight years,
                lone boatman on the night-blackened lake,
J-stroke and j-stroke, no end in sight,
One speck of return in my bad eye,
I breathe the mist off the dark waters, fragrance of what's-to-come.

———————

Winter begins unnoticed.
The way between half-empty and half-full
                begins where you begin forgetting the words,
And put down your pen.
The way to whatever matters begins after that.

POSTSCRIPTS

Little Apokatastasis

South of the stunned Rivanna, shadowless winter afternoon,
Light halfway on, clouds low-slung with rain-to-come
                                        stretched on the sky.

Window-watching, tangled branches across the lost highway, I
Suddenly see hundreds of headlights,
                              everyone coming home.

Star Turn III

Downloaded sky, color of wet cement,
Floaters like tiny stars wherever I cast my gaze,
Down here and up there.
                              I'm looking across the morning's Blue Ridge,
A snail's track of light where earth and clouds seam together.

Last week, snow on the slick limbs of the ginkgo tree.
                                                    Overnight,
Six inches or more.
If it were still water, the rivers would overflow
Their banks.
              And we'd be floating, lips, like free-range stars, in the sky.

———————

The turkey buzzards vortex and wheel
                                against the winter's blue tranquillity,
Contrails above them, bare branches under their tipped wings
North of the reservoir, east of town.
Meanwhile, the crows, like floating black stars,
                                        drag through the underwinds.

———————

Beautiful stars of the Big Dipper,
                        Orion's Belt and Cassiopeia
Sliding their canopy over the eastern December sky.
Like borrowed phrases, they ink our eyes.
Like patterns out of the deep past,
                            they splash us, they thrill our ears.

Stars are here when we come and stars are here when we go.
No one will ever know their secrets,

                              no one will break their codes,
So absent and all at once,

                    where all things are forgot.
Such useless change in our pants pockets, such dried flowers.

In Praise of Han Shan

Cold Mountain and Cold Mountain became the same thing in the
    mind,
The first last seen
                slipping into a crevice in the second.

Only the poems remained,
                    scrawled on the rocks and trees,
Nothing's undoing among the self-stung unfolding of things.

NOTES

"There Is a Balm in Gilead": *Mountain Home*, trans. David Hinton (New York: Counterpoint, 2002).

"Buffalo Yoga": Georg Trakl, *Poems*, trans. Lucia Getsi (Athens, Ohio: Mundus Artium Press, 1973); "L'Ame de Napoléon, 1912," by Leon Bloy, in Jorge Luis Borges, *Selected Non-Fictions*, ed. Eliot Weinberger (New York: Penguin Books, 1999).
Tom Andrews (1961–2001): "Alles Nahe werde fern" (Goethe).

"Rosso Venexiano":
Berryman: Well, being a poet is a funny kind of jazz. It doesn't get you anything. It doesn't get you any money, or not much, and it doesn't get you any prestige, or not much. It's just something you *do*.
Interviewer: Why?
Berryman: That's a tough question. I'll tell you a real answer. I'm taking your question seriously. This comes from Hamann, quoted by Kierkegaard. There are two voices, and the first voice says, "Write!" and the second voice says, "For whom?" I think that's marvelous; he doesn't question the imperative, you see that. And the first voice says, "For the dead whom thou didst love." Again the second voice doesn't question it; instead it says, "Will they read me?" And the first voice says, "Aye, for they return as posterity." Isn't that good?
—John Berryman, *Antæus*, #8, Winter 1973

"Sinology": *Mountain Home*.

"Little Apokatastasis": Apokatastasis: "That word promises reverse movement." Czeslaw Milosz, *Bells in Winter* (New York: Ecco Press, 1978).

"In Praise of Han Shan": *Mountain Home*.